J 658.408 MEY
Meyer, Terry Teague
Social entrepreneurship :
doing well while doing
good

101114

DIGITAL AND INFORMATION LITERACY ™

SOCIAL
ENTREPRENEURSHIP: DOING WELL WHILE DOING GOOD

TERRY TEAGUE MEYER

rosen publishing's
rosen central

Published in 2015 by The Rosen Publishing Group, Inc.
29 East 21st Street, New York, NY 10010

Library of Congress Cataloging-in-Publication Data

Meyer, Terry Teague.
Social entrepreneurship: doing well while doing good/Terry Teague Meyer. — First Edition.
     pages cm. — (Digital and information literacy)
Audience: Grades 5 to 8.
Includes bibliographical references and index.
ISBN 978-1-4777-7651-3 (library bound) — ISBN 978-1-4777-7653-7 (pbk.)
— ISBN 978-1-4777-7654-4 (6-pack)
1. Social entrepreneurship—Juvenile literature. I. Title.
HD60.M494 2014
658.4'08—dc23

                                                                    2014002137

Manufactured in the United States of America

CONTENTS

INTRODUCTION

What does South Carolina teen Katie Stagliano have in common with Bangladesh-born Nobel Prize winner Muhammad Yunus? Both are social entrepreneurs. Yunus founded the Grameen Bank and pioneered the idea of microlending—giving very small loans to needy individuals to help them start businesses and move out of poverty. Katie founded Katie's Krops to get other teens like herself to grow vegetables to donate to hungry people.

As the Internet and advances in telecommunications make people around the world feel closer to one another, more people are focusing on problems that once seemed far away. Seeing the problems in less developed countries through video, webcasts, and even two-way video communication like Skype has made many young people want to help those less fortunate. Today children and teens are looking for ways to help solve problems in their schools, neighborhoods, and around the world.

Solving big problems takes more than a desire to help others. It also takes energy, planning, and money. But these requirements don't discourage a particular type of young person—the social entrepreneur.

A social entrepreneur does many of the same things as philanthropists, people who donate their time and money to good causes. Social entrepreneurs identify problems in society, those close to home or far away, and

These Bangladeshi women salute their futures as successful entrepreneurs at a meeting to pay back their loans from Grameen Bank.

come up with creative solutions. Like business entrepreneurs who start new ventures in order to make a profit, social entrepreneurs must plan ahead to turn their ideas into working enterprises. Like all business owners, social entrepreneurs must find ways to get information and connect with people who will help them to meet their goals. They must seek markets—places to sell their service or product—and if they are making a product, they need to figure out how and where to make it, how much it will cost to make, and what they should charge for it. They must know how to publicize the project, and if they are successful, they must know what to do with the money they make.

A surprising number of young people have already done this. Some, like eighteen-year-olds Jared Kleinert and Logan Gardner, have developed websites with the aim of helping other young people become successful social entrepreneurs. Kleinert's business is the crowdfunding site Synergist, which helps to raise money for young social entrepreneurs. Gardner is the founder of Kids for Kids, a group that helps high school students develop the skills they need to launch their own social entrepreneurship projects.

The growth of the social entrepreneurship movement goes hand in hand with the growing ease in connection and communication made possible by digital advancements. Clearly, it's easier to communicate an idea to more people through the Internet than by word of mouth. Computers, portable digital devices, social networking, crowdfunding, and other digital equipment and technologies make it possible for social entrepreneurs to solve problems far from their own neighborhoods. However, starting a business for any purpose requires planning, organization, and information beyond what is taught in schools. This resource contains detailed information about using current technology and online information that can help a young person like you turn dreams of a better world into reality. Solving social problems close to home or across the globe is easier with the information and resources to plan ahead, organize a team, get the word out, and find the money needed to make it happen.

Chapter 1

Could You Be a Social Entrepreneur?

What is a social entrepreneur?

An entrepreneur is someone who organizes and runs a business, often risking his or her own money to start up a new venture. Social entrepreneurs are people whose business is to provide the money or a product that will solve big or small problems close to home or far away.

Many social entrepreneurs work for causes through nonprofit organizations. These kinds of organizations use the money they make to support their cause. They do not use the money for the financial gain of the business owners. But working for a good cause doesn't necessarily mean it's impossible or wrong to make a profit. Some businesses can do good in the community while still doing well for themselves financially. For example, Grameen Bank in Bangladesh helps the poor get small loans. This means people who would not get a loan from most banks now have money that they can put to good use. When the loans are paid back, the bank makes a profit.

The term "social entrepreneurship" is only about twenty-five years old, but people who have started businesses to help others is a very old concept.

Young people are helping solve big problems by working together through organizations like generationOn Service Clubs.

Maria Montessori opened a school in 1907 and changed the world of education for very young children. Florence Nightingale started a nursing school that taught many modern nursing practices and saved countless lives. The recent boom in social entrepreneurship has been encouraged by organizations such as Ashoka, Echoing Green, the Skoll Foundation, and the Draper Richards Foundation. They provide training and start-up funding for social entrepreneurs. Organizations like these support ventures, often called "initiatives," because they have new methods to tackle global problems like hunger, disease, abuse of people and animals, and damage to the environment.

File   Edit   View   Favorites   Tools   Help

WHAT INSPIRED THESE SOCIAL ENTREPRENEURS?

What Inspired These Social Entrepreneurs?

Taylor Crabtree was only seven when she realized that not only people like her grandmother but also many children were battling cancer. Wanting to help cheer and comfort young cancer victims, she came up with the idea for what became the TayBear company. She began decorating plain hair clasps to sell in order to buy teddy bears to donate to young cancer patients. Each bear was given a name.

Katie's Krops, an organization to combat hunger by getting young people gardening, began when ten-year-old Katie Stagliano grew a forty pound (eighteen kilogram) cabbage and decided to donate it to a local soup kitchen. It was then that she realized the extent of hunger in her area and decided to use her love of gardening to do something about it.

The nonprofit Sight Learning was created when California teen Yash Gupta broke his glasses during the first week of high school. Being without glasses for a week made him realize how important good vision is to learning. When he found out that twelve million children worldwide are without the glasses they need, he started collecting and distributing used glasses. His nonprofit organization has since donated over $500,000 in eyeglasses to students around the world.

This cuddly bear is one of thousands given to children with cancer through TayBear.

These organizations recognize that young people can effect change and are spreading the movement by offering programs and training to involve young people. They also provide models and online tool kits that make it easier for beginning social entrepreneurs to become effective quickly.

What's the Big Idea?

Becoming a social entrepreneur actually involves two big ideas: the problem and the solution. Finding problems that need fixing is not difficult. Ideally, the focus of an effort to make a social impact should be a personal choice, since following through on a project and convincing others to support it requires strong commitment to the cause. Some people may read about a situation or hear about it through the media and instantly feel called to help out. Others should focus on their natural interests and talents.

Providing solutions to society's problems doesn't necessarily mean simply giving products or services to those who need them. Microlending is an important area of social entrepreneurship. Microlenders such as Kiva offer very small loans (as little as $100) to people who need money but who would have trouble getting a loan otherwise. The loans are used to start business ventures. Examples include things like enabling someone to plant a garden and sell the produce for profit. A woman in an African village might be able to buy a cow or goat in order to start raising animals for dairy products. As with a normal bank loan, the borrower pays back the lender with interest, increasing the amount available to make new loans.

Designing products that the poor can afford is another focus of social entrepreneurs. For example, professors and students at the Stanford University School of Design work with people in impoverished areas to design needed products like water pumps, incubators, and electric lighting that can be sold for as little as $30.

Problems that need attention are everywhere. There might be one in your own school, neighborhood, or city. You can join the efforts of churches and civic organizations such as Rotary International and Scouting that are already involved in helping others. The Internet is also a valuable resource for

These young people won awards from DoSomething.org for their social enterprises. The 2013 awards ceremony was televised on VH1.

beginning social entrepreneurs. Websites like TakingITGlobal, DoSomething .org, YesKidzCan!, and Girl's CEO Connection can make it easy for you to identify and get started on worthy projects.

Finding a solution is a harder but very important step for social entrepreneurs. Following a natural disaster, you might organize volunteers to conduct a food or clothing drive to help victims, or like Taylor Crabtree, you might start a business to earn money for your cause. Look at what Canadian high school senior Akash Gupta did. He wanted to make his town, Fort McMurray, Alberta, a greener and more sustainable community. So he joined with friends to create a company called the Great Green North, which sells composting kits. He developed a business plan, set goals, and issued checks to people who had invested in his business, all while going to school and helping out with his family's construction business. In 2013, Gupta interviewed computer tech entrepreneur Josh Kopelman, who had advice for young people looking to start a new venture. Kopelman recommends keeping a journal of the three best and worst things about their day. He explains that the best ideas for new ventures often involve solving an issue or inconvenience. A journal can help to identify issues and help to focus on the solution.

The best solutions will make use of your interests and talents. Taylor Crabtree had experience making decorative hair clasps when she decided to sell them to support young cancer patients. Katie Stagliano was already a gardener when she grew her giant cabbage. In his book *Social Entrepreneurship*, David Bornstein lists two initial "thoughts for changemakers": first, "begin with an end in mind," and second, "do what you do best." Think about what you are interested in and good at doing. If you love animals, you might work to help homeless animals or protect endangered animal habitats. If you are very friendly, you can use your natural social skills for fund-raising.

Being a social entrepreneur requires a thoughtful plan. Think about the overall goal of the project. How, in practical terms, will the project work toward reaching that goal? A brainstorming session with the help of peers and adults can help you figure this out. Consider how much time you can devote to the project. Think about how long it will take to reach your goal. Now you are ready to look at the details.

To run a successful social venture, there are many smaller details to consider. How many others and how much money will you need to get things started? How will day-to-day operations be funded and managed? Will the project raise money through special events, sale of products, fund-raisers, auctions, or something else? How will the project or organization spend the money it raises? How will it attract, manage, and keep donors and volunteers on board? These may seem like tough questions, but the same organizations that can help identify areas of need can also provide tool kits with detailed information about taking a project from start to finish. YesKidzCan! is aimed at younger children and their parents and offers complete information about a number of varied projects—including templates for art projects and recipes for dog treats to donate to an animal shelter. For someone wanting to start a project of their own, this site offers a good model of the details involved in planning a social enterprise.

Once you know these main details, try shrinking your big idea into a short message. Early on in the planning process is the time to begin crafting an "elevator pitch." This is an idea that can be clearly explained in the few minutes it takes to ride an elevator. People today are used to sales pitches in the form of television and Internet ads. An elevator pitch must be short and interesting so that people won't tune it out. The message should present the "why" and the "how" of the project as simply as possible. It should also show your enthusiasm for the cause. This short message can be used for your venture's mission statement. This explains your company's goals and how you will achieve them. It is the foundation of a business plan.

MYTHS&FACTS

MYTH Only rich people and politicians can bring about social change.

FACT Young people, individuals, and groups working together are solving problems around the world. *NBC Nightly News* often includes a segment called "Making a Difference," and *People* magazine regularly features "Heroes Among Us." These and other media outlets highlight what regular people can accomplish through inspiration and determination.

MYTH It's impossible to fit social entrepreneurship into a school schedule.

FACT Many young people have shown that they can do big things while still in school. You may have to give up some activities to make time for a project, but the project itself may offer social interaction and the chance to meet new people along with a sense of accomplishment. If starting a project of your own seems too time-consuming, find an existing organization in your area of interest and volunteer during school vacations.

MYTH Social entrepreneurs can't make a profit.

FACT While some social enterprises make money only to support a given cause, others may make a profit while fulfilling a worthy mission. Coffee shops run by Youth Ventures in Staples and East Saint Paul, Minnesota, create and provide jobs and business training and work experience to young people, as well as a welcoming place for the community to connect and socialize. Another organization, Back to the Roots, supports the environment by using a waste product (coffee grounds from commercial shops) to create kits used to grow gourmet mushrooms in people's homes. Both companies make a profit.

Chapter 2

Building a Team

ne person can have the idea to bring about real change, but it takes a team to turn the idea into an enterprise. The beginning social entrepreneur should start by looking to family, friends, and teachers for help. An experienced guide and counselor is also helpful. A mentor can fill this role. A mentor is an adviser who helps someone who is new to a school, business, or other organization. A good mentor might already know something about the cause or about running a business. A science teacher could be a good source for an environmental or recycling project. A business or computer instructor could offer needed expertise about raising and managing money and setting up a website. Coaches, band leaders, clergy, and scout leaders all have experience in fund-raising and organizing volunteers. You could look for a mentor through organizations focused on similar problems. By volunteering at a local animal rescue center, for example, you could observe how the organization operates and probably find an adult mentor with experience in this area of interest.

A bolder approach would be to contact someone well-known who understands the cause or has political or economic power. The National

Working together, twenty-five teachers and students at Alton High School in Godfrey, Illinois, raised over $5,000 for cancer research in a one day event.

Mentoring Partnership (MENTOR) can also help young people find mentors among local volunteers. Remember that elevator pitch? Now is the time to use it. Practice presenting a clear and persuasive argument for your cause to people you know before seeking help and money from strangers.

File   Edit   View   Favorites   Tools   Help

      PROFILE OF A SUCCESSFUL TEAM

Profile of a Successful Team

Back to the Roots is a green enterprise that has received many awards and been featured on television shows dealing with business, ecology, and food. The company was founded by Alejandro Velez and Nikhil Arora when they were seniors at the University of California at Berkeley. They met and got the idea for their company during a business class when a professor mentioned that it might be possible to grow gourmet mushrooms using only used coffee grounds. The pair teamed up and began experimenting, making ten batches of mushrooms. Nine of the batches failed, but their one success led to the creation of a thriving business selling mushroom growing kits. The kits use material that would otherwise end up in landfills to provide fresh homegrown mushrooms. The company is paid to collect coffee grounds from local shops. After they use the coffee grounds, they donate what is left to local farmers or sell it to be used to improve garden soil. Interviewed on PBS *BizKid$*, Arora said, "You can be green and make green." Part of the company's mission is to "make food personal again." Following the success of their sustainable mushroom growing operation, the company has developed a fish tank that uses fish waste to feed edible plants while the plants keep the fishes' water clean!

Back to the Roots mushroom growing kits use old coffee grounds to produce mushrooms—and a good profit.

Working Together Multiplies Results

Part of researching a new venture should be to determine whether someone else is already working on the same thing and whether there is room for more entrants in the field. If there is, what would be the best way to complement, enhance, or coordinate the effort? In the world of for-profit business, competitors offering similar products and services may compete for customers and try to drive each other out of business. Social entrepreneurs working toward the same or similar goals need to complement each others' efforts to build a wider community. Working for an existing social enterprise can be a great opportunity to learn about day-to-day operations, to meet like-minded people, and to find a mentor.

File   Edit   View   Favorites   Tools   Help

HOW ONE ORGANIZATION HELPS SOCIAL ENTREPRENEURS

How One Organization Helps Social Entrepreneurs

Founded in 1999, TakingITGlobal is a social network whose purpose is to involve young people around the world in worthwhile causes. The organization's website focuses on social innovation, global education, and bringing together like-minded young people through digital connections. The digital community enables members to share stories and discuss issues that are important to them. A member can find and connect with others based on location, interests, language, and more. The TakingITGlobal site has links to many resources and a tool kit to help young social entrepreneurs organize and spread the word about their initiatives. The organization also provides educational support in the form of resources, online courses, and even games. TakingITGlobal works with other organizations that share its goals.

Collaboration (working together to do or create something) is often a faster way to meet goals. In addition to your family, friends, and mentors, try reaching out to the community. Local newspapers are always looking for interesting features about people in the area. Offering an interview or writing a press release that explains what your business is about could bring collaborators from local businesses or find additional volunteers and donations.

Another important way to connect with possible collaborators is through social entrepreneurship organizations and foundations, such as the Case

French finance minister Christine Lagarde (*right*) meets with young Global Changemakers from around the world at a conference in Davos, Switzerland, in 2011.

Foundation, Idealist.org, and others previously mentioned. Bringing people together across cyberspace is only one of the ways such organizations help solve social and environmental problems

For those interested in social enterprises to solve problems in distant countries, online resources such as OneWorld.org and Changemakers .com can help. The University of Pennsylvania's site kwhs.wharton.upenn.edu (Wharton@Knowledge High School) provides current articles on young social entrepreneurs and helpful links to organizations that support such causes. There is also an online newspaper, the *Chronicle of Philanthropy,* that covers news of nonprofit organizations.

Chapter 3

Making a Plan

A business plan is essential for any venture, even a social enterprise. It gives you and others involved in your venture a map of how the business will be run. In the process of creating a business plan, you get a chance to act out what the business will do, which will help you to figure out whether or not it can succeed before you spend much time or money. As you act out how the business will run, the important thing is to ensure you can make enough money to continue and possibly to expand operations. Any profit would be used either to pay for donations for the chosen project or to keep the enterprise going.

The business plan should provide answers to a number of essential questions. What makes my product or service unique? Is there a market for it—or who will use my product or service? How do I decide on an appropriate price for goods and services sold to raise funds for the organization? How much money will be needed to start up the venture? When will it begin to make a profit (or become self-supporting)? What kind of expertise is needed to successfully run the venture? How many people are needed to keep the venture going? What are the best ways to market and publicize the organization?

Getting Help from the Small Business Administration

The Small Business Administration (SBA) is a federal service that offers online courses and videos with detailed information about making a business plan. The SBA website Teen Business Link (http://www.sbaonline.sba.gov/teens) is easy to use and provides helpful links and examples of business plans for both services and sales-oriented ventures. The SBA website also includes a tool to help you create a business plan. The process is step by step and includes definitions of terms and examples of things you may need to include in your plan, like product descriptions and market research. The

The U.S. Small Business Administration Teen Business Link provides help in creating a business plan and carrying it out.

SBA can help the young entrepreneur with online information about loans and grants and a course on crowdfunding—an online collective effort to pool money for a particular project. By registering with the SBA online community, business newcomers can find help and read blogs with advice from experienced entrepreneurs. The SBA has many local offices to provide help in person. Through the nonprofit organization SCORE, they can connect people with business mentors. Although the SBA does not offer advice to social entrepreneurs in particular, its business information is invaluable to anyone just getting started.

The SBA tool for making a business plan assumes that the business plan will project company activities for three to five years. That may not be practical for a young person still in school or for projects that are focused on a one-time event. A young social entrepreneur should envision growth and success from the very start. A one-time event could become an annual event and a successful social enterprise could continue to thrive long after its founder has gone off to college.

What a business plan might include:

1. A simple statement of purpose and goals. This might be the expanded version of your elevator pitch. This statement is the foundation of a business plan and should show the social entrepreneur's passion for his or her cause. It will be used to recruit other participants, get donations, and convince consumers to buy a product or service.

2. A description of the product, service, or event. From this description, the entrepreneur should be able to come up with a list of needs and costs to create the product or run the service or event.

For a product:
What materials are needed, and what is the cost of materials?
How many versions will be made? How much time is needed to make it?
How and where will it be marketed?

What is the means of distribution?
What is the product's price?

For an event:
What is the location and date for an event?
How much are rental costs?
How many volunteers will prepare and carry out the event?

3. Personnel: These are the people you will need to carry out the project. How many will help to start the project, and how many will you need as the project grows? Is it possible to depend on volunteers only, or will you need to pay for help? For example, one might need

It takes a team. These students are supporting the K-9 unit of the local Fairfield County, Ohio, sheriff's department through a doggie treat fund-raiser.

skills and equipment for carpentry and electrical work, sewing, or food preparation.

4. Legal considerations. The SBA Teen Business Link includes links to federal agencies that cover a range of important business concerns. The Internal Revenue Service has information about filing for an Employment Identification Number (which is sort of like a Social Security number for businesses and organizations). This allows your business to conduct financial transactions, like paying employees, banking, and becoming eligible for tax-exempt status. Other links are related to how your business is organized (for example, who is responsible for which activities), labor laws, copyrights, and patents. In

Publicity and marketing are essential considerations in putting together a social enterprise business plan.

addition to federal legal concerns, local government may require you to get a license to run your business.

5. Start-up costs. These include things like the raw materials needed to make products and rental costs associated with an event.

6. Publicity and marketing. How will you get the word out and convince people to buy your product, use your service, or participate in your event? To a certain extent, marketing should be one of the first things to think about when considering an idea, since the enterprise will not be successful if people don't know about it or are just not interested.

In addition, publicity is needed at every step, to recruit volunteers who will help bring the project to a reality, bring in donations, and get the word

Your Local Expert, the Librarian!

Since online resources change and increase in number so rapidly, it's often difficult to find the best ones easily. For help, look to the librarian at your school or local library or to a helpful list of the annual Best Websites for Teaching and Learning, compiled annually by the American Association of School Librarians. Among the top sites listed for 2013 is WorkFlowy, a free site that can be used to help an individual organize and prioritize tasks and help groups collaborate on projects by making it easier to share information and by making specific work assignments. A librarian is professionally trained in research techniques and can show how to access databases and use search engines more effectively.

out to likely customers. That is why it is essential to define one's goals and vision early on.

Pay special attention to the role of social media in sharing ideas and promoting business as you create your business plan. Which type of social media—Facebook, Twitter, YouTube, Pinterest—is most likely to serve the needs of the project? Recognize that new venues and platforms are always cropping up. Trying to be a presence on too many sites might make it difficult to update frequently enough to keep people interested. Look for the places where the people who need your product or service, or are interested in your cause, spend their online time. Then use that venue for online promotion.

Don't worry if the SBA business plan ideas seem too complicated. They are simply models that can save you time and frustration in the long run. Realistically, fear of making a business plan should not stand in the way of starting a social enterprise. On her website, Taylor Crabtree mentions that she learned about business as she worked on her venture. She learned to use Quicken accounting software, a product that helps businesses manage money, early on. She states, "I just learned what I needed to know to be able to do what I needed to do when I needed to do it." That plan could work for anyone.

Chapter 4

Where's the Money?

There are basically three ways to fund a social enterprise: ask for donations through fund-raising or crowdfunding, borrow money from a bank, or generate income by selling goods or services. Many social entrepreneurs use a combination of methods.

Familiar Sources Close to Home

Even those planning to earn money for their project will need some money to get started. Since most ventures take time to become profitable or even self-supporting, it's wise to start with enough money to keep things going. The amount needed and for how long should be part of the business plan. Depending on the amount needed, young people may be able to use savings or borrow from family or friends. However, any loans arranged informally (meaning a nonbank loan) should include an agreement in writing. Any entrepreneur also needs some sort of banking arrangement. Depending on where you live, someone over age eighteen may be needed to open a bank account for storing funds and making payments.

Someone under the age of eighteen may need to partner with an adult in order to set up banking arrangements for a project.

Keeping Track

No matter how you get your first start-up money, it's important to start keeping records and saving receipts immediately. This will help you to track how money is being used. If your project includes transportation costs, like going out to buy materials or getting people to a location, mileage or public transportation costs could be tax deductible. This reduces how much money your company pays in taxes, which would free up more money to be used for the social enterprise. Keeping track of how money is spent, miles traveled, and

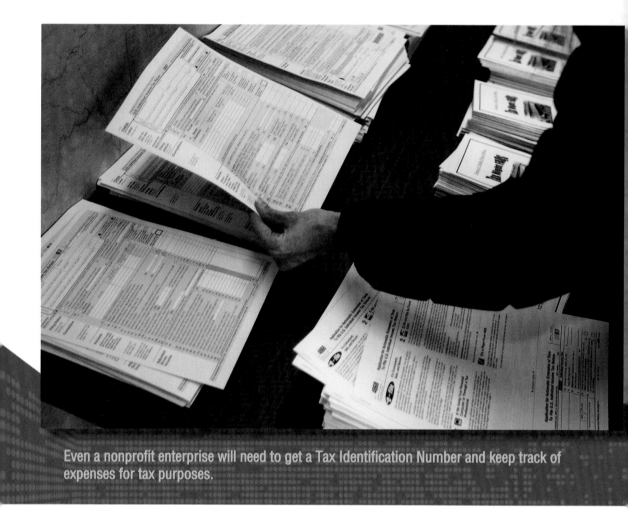

Even a nonprofit enterprise will need to get a Tax Identification Number and keep track of expenses for tax purposes.

even volunteer hours may also help to show how well you run your business and can help you to secure funding to support and build your social enterprise.

Grants and Loans

A grant is money that you can apply for that you do not have to pay back. A loan, however, must be paid back to the institution you borrowed it from, often with interest. Check with local churches, businesses, the chamber of commerce,

File   Edit   View   Favorites   Tools   Help

      CROWDSOURCING AND CROWDFUNDING

Crowdsourcing and Crowdfunding

Crowdsourcing refers to the practice of reaching out for ideas and services from a large group of people in the online community. Social media enables social entrepreneurs to reach a larger crowd than they might through other methods. Examples of crowdsourcing are when organizations invite people to enter a photo, slogan, or advertising video to be judged by a vote from the online crowd.

Crowdfunding uses social media to find individuals willing to pool their money for a project. The project's owner usually offers an incentive for people to donate, like access to a limited edition product or first access to an event. Crowdfunding typically runs for a limited span of time. Well established platforms for crowdfunding include Indiegogo, RocketHub, Kickstarter, and RockThePost. Devin Thorpe, who raised money for his book on social entrepreneurship using StartSomeGood.com, recommends this and several other sites as especially good for social entrepreneurs. Kicking off a crowdfunding project can be a lot of work, but sites like Fundly.com, currently the largest site for nonprofits and social entrepreneurs, offers packages of social media programs that eliminate some of the work.

In a *Forbes* article, Tanya Prive, cofounder of RockThePost, explains that each crowdfunding site offers something unique, yet they all have much in common. The individual or organization typically submits a profile and video introduction to the project along with a list of rewards per donation. The idea is to create a means to draw the attention of likely contributors and to make them want to become a supporter. Prive emphasizes the impor-tance of a video that will grab people. However, she also stresses the importance of spreading the word through personal and social media

(continued on next page)

CROWDSOURCING AND CROWDFUNDING

contacts before launching the crowdfunding project.

Crowdfunding sites are not free. Funding.com, for example, takes a percentage of what is raised. PiggyBackr, aimed at young people raising funds for all sorts of reasons (not necessarily social entrepreneurs), charges either a percentage or a subscription fee. The cost and payment arrangement depends on the site. Deciding whether or not to use crowdfunding and which site to use is an important part of the business plan.

Zach Vorhies, creator of Zackees cycling turn-signal gloves, raised $35,000 with Kickstarter. His invention makes cycling safer by making cyclists more visible to motorists.

and organizations such as Rotary International and Scouting. They may have programs set up to provide grants or loans for worthy projects. Applying for either a grant or a loan will involve detailed paperwork. This is where a good business plan and tracking how money has been spent can help you. The granting organization (called the granter) will definitely expect to get back evidence of exactly how the money was used. The granter will probably include information about keeping records along with the grant application.

Granters may require applicants to have nonprofit status and have been in operation for a certain length of time (three years is typical). The World We Want Foundation funds initiatives from young people, who must partner with an existing tax-exempt nonprofit. Writing a grant proposal can be very complicated, but there are some kid-friendly programs. For example,

The World We Want Foundation is among many organizations that provide grants and assistance to launch social enterprises and help them succeed.

Katie's Krops started with help from the Launch My Dream program from AmazingKids.

Becoming an Official Nonprofit

Setting up your venture as a nonprofit is important because it determines the amount of taxes the organization must pay. For-profit business ventures are taxed based on their profit. This is how much they make after deducting the costs of running the business. Nonprofits, on the other hand, do not pay federal taxes. Typically, donations made to nonprofits are also tax-fee. The IRS website has complete instructions with forms and requirements for becoming tax exempt. The process requires time and paperwork, so for those eager to get up and running, tax exempt status is probably not a primary concern, but it would be wise to check into the process early on.

Chapter 5

What Happens Next?

Several of the successful social enterprises profiled here have grown beyond what their founders probably envisioned at the beginning. National media attention and awards focused attention on such worthy projects and undoubtedly helped them become even more successful. But each of them started small.

"Start small and aim to grow" is a good motto for those who want to bring about positive changes in the world. Planning ahead means breaking bigger ideas into small tasks that can be completed now and in the future. What those tasks are depends on the nature of the individual project.

Social enterprises can fulfill several community needs. There is the group of coffee shops that adults and teens in Staples, a small, low-income town in Minnesota, worked to open. It took several years of work before the first coffee shop was ready for customers. The organizers held weekly planning meetings. They raised money, partly through grants. They prepared menus and learned to use equipment. They even painted and decorated the spaces. In the process, the young people involved gained a valuable education in business and entrepreneurial skills. When the coffee houses opened, they provided money and work experience for the teen employees and a

Through the organization Urban Roots, young people learn gardening and business skills while providing fresh produce for their community.

place for community members to come together and socialize. Those who participated in these projects expect that they will continue to provide jobs for local young people and a stronger sense of community among local residents.

A different type of project in East Saint Paul, Minnesota, involves young people working through Urban Roots, which grows and markets affordable, fresh food for people in a low-income urban community. They manage a number of gardens and sell the produce through farm share programs and at outdoor markets. Their daily activities change seasonally, from planning the gardens to marketing their vegetables and flowers. Like the coffee shops, this social enterprise also provides training and employment for youth. It also provides fresh, healthy food for the community.

Social entrepreneurship takes so many forms that it's impossible to mention all the ways a venture might turn out. For some, meeting a crowdfunding goal might be the end of a project. When the money is used for its intended purpose, the project is completed. For others, this funding would be start-up

Soccer players at Bay City Western High School in Auburn, Michigan, use their game as an opportunity to raise funds for the American Cancer Society.

money to launch a project or product. For some, like the founders of Back to the Roots, the start-up might become an enterprise with several employees and plans for the future. The Minnesota coffee shops and urban gardens are ongoing ventures that continue to benefit the communities they serve.

There is no guarantee that a social enterprise will raise thousands of dollars and touch thousands of lives. But a social enterprise is bound to change the life of the person who undertakes it. He or she is showing the willingness to use time, creativity, effort, and money to help others in need and nurture the environment that supports them.

TEN GREAT QUESTIONS

TO ASK A SOCIAL ENTREPRENEUR

1   How and where do you find worthy causes to support?

2   How do you come up with project ideas to raise money for a cause?

3   What are the best ways to raise money to start a business venture?

4   How do you break down big problems into smaller tasks that can be accomplished?

5   How can I find a mentor?

6   How does one recruit volunteers to get a project started and keep it going?

7   What are the advantages and disadvantages of using social media to publicize my project?

8   What is involved in getting grant money?

9   What business activities (like banking, for example) will require help from adults?

10   How can I manage my time in order to keep up with school work and my social venture?

GLOSSARY

business venture A business enterprise involving risk.

collaborators People or organizations that work with someone to complete a project.

elevator pitch A brief, clear presentation of an idea covering all of its important points (short enough that it can be delivered in the length of an elevator ride).

enterprise A business or company; a project.

entrepreneur A person who organizes and operates a business or project.

foundation A nonprofit organization that either donates funds and support to other organizations or provides funding for its own charitable purposes.

funding Money provided for a particular purpose.

grant Money provided to support a project. A grant does not need to be repaid.

green Used to refer to something that is helpful (or not harmful) to the environment.

initiative An act or plan meant to resolve a problem or improve a situation.

marketing Promoting and selling products or services.

mission statement A description of the goals of an organization and how it intends to fulfill them.

nonprofit An enterprise whose purpose is to support a cause, rather than to make money.

philanthropy The desire to help others, expressed by donating time or money to good causes.

profit Money that is made by a business after all costs and expenses are paid.

recruit To get someone to join an organization or support a cause.

FOR MORE INFORMATION

Ashoka
1700 North Moore Street
Suite 2000
Arlington, VA 22209
(703) 527-8300
Website: https://www.ashoka.org
Ashoka is the world's largest association of leading social entrepreneurs,
    with world headquarters in the Washington, D.C., area and regional
    offices around the world. The organization sponsors a number of initia-
    tives and programs including Changemakers and Youth Venture, Inc.

The Canadian Social Entrepreneurship Foundation
1480 Garnet Road, Unit 7
Victoria, BC V8P 5K9
Canada
(250) 891-2209
Website: http://www.csef.ca
The Canadian Social Entrepreneurship Foundation exists to educate, recog-
    nize, and fund existing social entrepreneurs and encourage new social
    enterprises in Canada and around the world. The foundation sponsors
    an online ideas challenge to encourage participants to come up with
    promising solutions to big problems.

MENTOR (National Mentoring Partnership)
201 South Street, Sixth Floor
Boston, MA 02111
(617) 303-4600

Website: http://www.mentoring.org
MENTOR encourages adults throughout the country to become mentors and,
     through local partnerships, matches young people with mentors.

TakingITGlobal
19 Duncan Street, Suite 505
Toronto, ON M5H 3H1
Canada
(416) 977-9363
Website: http://www.tigweb.org
This Canadian organization has worldwide reach. TakingITGlobal supports
     young social entrepreneurs by providing education and digital connec-
     tions and sponsoring a number of platforms for social innovation.

U.S. Small Business Administration (SBA)
409 3rd Street SW
Washington, DC 20416
(800) 827-5722
Website: http://www.sba.gov
The SBA assists small businesses with education, information, technical
     assistance, and training. The agency also provides financing and
     opportunities to get government contracts.

VolunteerMatch
550 Montgomery Street, 8th Floor
San Francisco, CA 94111
(415) 241-6868

Website: http://www.volunteermatch.org
VolunteerMatch connects volunteers with organizations that need help. The
    website helps volunteers find organizations in their geographic area
    and area of interest. The organization also provides education and
    information about running a nonprofit.

Websites

Due to the changing nature of Internet links, Rosen Publishing has developed
an online list of websites related to the subject of this book. This site is
updated regularly. Please use this link to access the list:

http://www.rosenlinks.com/DIL/entre

FOR FURTHER READING

Aaker, Jennifer, and Andy Smith. *The Dragonfly Effect: Quick, Effective, and Powerful Ways to Use Social Media to Drive Social Change*. San Francisco, CA: Jossey-Bass, 2010.

Burrows, Terry. *Blogs, Wikis, MySpace, and More: Everything You Want to Know About Using Web 2.0 but Are Afraid to Ask*. Chicago, IL: Chicago Review Press, 2008.

DaSilva-Gordon, Maria. *Top 10 Secrets for Making Money and Even More Money*. New York, NY: Rosen Publishing, 2014.

Furgang, Kathy. *Money-Making Opportunities for Teens Who Are Computer Savvy*. New York, NY: Rosen Publishing, 2014.

Hansen, Mark Victor. *The Richest Kids in America: How They Earn It, How They Spend It, How You Can Too*. Newport Beach, CA: Hansen House Publishing, 2009.

Hollander, Barbara Gottfried. *The Next Big Thing: Developing Your Digital Business Idea*. New York, NY: Rosen Publishing, 2013.

Johnson, Arne, and Karen Macklin. *Indie Girl: From Starting a Band to Launching a Fashion Company, Nine Ways to Turn Your Creative Talent into Reality*. San Francisco, CA: Zest Books/Orange Avenue Publishing, 2008.

MacMillan, Ian C., and James D. Thompson. *The Social Entrepreneur's Playbook, Expanded Edition*. Philadelphia, PA: Wharton Digital Press, 2013.

McCrea, Jennifer, and Jeffrey C. Walker. *The Generosity Network: New Transformational Tools for Successful Fund-Raising*. New York, NY: Deepak Chopra Books, 2013.

Mycoskie, Blake. *Start Something That Matters*. New York, NY: Spiegel & Grau, 2011.

O'Reilly, Tim, and Sarah Milstein. *The Twitter Book*. Sebastopol, CA: O'Reilly Media, 2009.

Polak, Paul, and Mal Warwick. *The Business Solution to Poverty: Designing Products and Services for Three Billion New Customers*. San Francisco, CA: Berrett-Koehler Publishers, 2013.

Rankin, Kenrya. *Start It Up: The Complete Teen Business Guide to Turning Your Passions Into Pay*. San Francisco, CA: Zest Books/Orange Avenue Publishing, 2011.

Selfridge, Benjamin. *A Teen's Guide to Creating Web Pages and Blogs*. Waco, TX: Prufrock Press, 2009.

Suen, Anastasia. *Internships & Volunteer Opportunities for People Who Love All Things Digital*. New York, NY: Rosen Publishing, 2013.

Thomases, Hollis. *Twitter Marketing: An Hour a Day*. Indianapolis, IN: Wiley Publishing, 2010.

Wilkinson, Colin. *Going Live: Launching Your Digital Business*. New York, NY: Rosen Publishing, 2013.

Ziolkowski, Jim. *Walk in Their Shoes: Can One Person Change the World?* New York, NY: Simon & Schuster, 2013.

Arrillaga-Andreessen, Laura. *Giving 2.0: Transform Your Giving and Our World*. San Francisco, CA: Jossey-Bass, 2012.

Bailey, Moira, and Diane Herbst. "Katie Stagliano Feeds the Hungry Through Her Gardening Nonprofit." *People*, December 12, 2013. Retrieved October 15, 2013 (http://www.people.com/people/article /0,,20647258,00.html).

Berry, Tim. "5 Ways to Start a Business Plan." SBA.gov, September 25, 2013. Retrieved October 19,2013 (http://www.sba.gov/community /blogs/5-ways-start-business-plan).

Bornstein, David, and Susan Davis. *Social Entrepreneurship: What Everyone Needs to Know*. New York, NY: Oxford University Press, 2010.

Clarke, Erika, and Kathleen Toner. "Teen's Vision: Help Kids See Clearer." CNN. Retrieved November 1, 2013 (http://www.cnn.com/2013 /09/05/health/cnnheroes-gupta-glasses/index.html).

Dailymotion. "BizKid$_Social Entrepreneurs." Retrieved July 1, 2013 (http://www.dailymotion.com/video/xztccu_biz-kid-social-entrepreneurs_lifestyle).

Durieux, Mark B., and Robert A. Stebbins. *Social Entrepreneurship for Dummies*. Hoboken, NJ: Wiley Publishing, 2010.

Howe, Jeff. *Crowdsourcing: Why the Power of the Crowd Is Driving the Future of Business*. New York, NY: Crown Business, 2008.

Johnson, Caitlin A. "High School Hero Comforts Kids with Cancer." CBS News, February 11, 2009. Retrieved September 15, 2013 (http:// www.cbsnews.com/2100-500178_162-2142481.html).

Knowledge@WhartonHighSchool. "The Power to Lead: The Next Generation of Social Entrepreneurs." Retrieved July 25, 2013 (http://kwhs.wharton .upenn.edu/2012/05/the-power-to-lead-the-next-generation-of-social-entrepreneurs).

Mook, Laurie, ed. *Businesses with a Difference: Balancing the Social and the Economic*. Toronto, ON, Canada: University of Toronto Press, 2012.

Partidge, Kenneth, ed. *Social Networking*. New York, NY: H.W. Wilson Company, 2011.

Prive, Tanya. "What Is Crowdfunding and How Does It Benefit the Economy." *Forbes*. Retrieved October 12, 2013 (http://www.forbes.com/sites/tanyaprive/2012/11/27/what-is-crowdfunding-and-how-does-it-benefit-the-economy).

Read, Stuart. *Effectual Entrepreneurship*. New York, NY: Routledge, 2011.

Scearce, Diana. "Working Wikily." *Stanford Social Innovation Review*. Retrieved August 2, 2013 (http://www.ssireview.org/articles/entry/working_wikily).

Scofield, Rupert. *The Social Entrepreneur's Handbook*. New York, NY: McGraw-Hill, 2011.

Tapscott, Don. *Grown Up Digital: How the New Generation Is Changing Your World*. New York, NY: McGraw-Hill, 2010.

Thorpe, Devin. "Eight Crowdfunding Sites for Social Entrepreneurs." *Forbes*. Retrieved August 10, 2013 (http://www.forbes.com/sites/devinthorpe/2012/09/10/eight-crowdfunding-sites-for-social-entrepreneurs).

Thorpe, Devin. "These Teenagers Are the Definition of Social Entrepreneur. Watch and Be Inspired." *Forbes*, April 12, 2013. Retrieved July 25, 2013 (http://www.forbes.com/sites/devinthorpe/2013/04/12/these-teenagers-are-the-definition-of-social-entrepreneur-watch-and-be-inspired).

Twin Cities Public Television. "Changemakers: Teens Who Earn and Learn." January 16, 2011. Retrieved September 15, 2013 (http://www.tpt.org/?a=programs&id=20973).

INDEX

About the Author

Writer and educator Terry Teague Meyer lives in Houston, Texas. She is a retired French teacher who has lived and traveled around the world. She supports social change by volunteering as a mentor and teacher of English as a second language.

Photo Credits

Cover and p. 1 (from left) © iStockphoto.com/mangostock, © iStockphoto .com/iqoncept, © iStockphoto.com/RapidEye, © iStockphoto.com/AVAVA; p. 5 Karen Kasmauski/Science Faction/Getty Images; p. 8 Jonathan Leibson /Getty Images; p. 9 Photo by Sean DuFrene/SDU-T/ZUMA Press, © Copyright 2006 by SDU-T; p. 11 Kevin Winter/Getty Images; pp. 16, 19, 24, 25, 37 © AP Images; p. 17 Justin Sullivan/Getty Images; p. 29 Blend Images /Ariel Skelley/Vetta/Getty Images; p. 30 Chris Hondros/Getty Images; p. 32 Rex Features/AP Images; p. 33 Britta Pedersen/picture-alliance/dpa/AP Images; p. 36 Urban Roots MN; cover (background) and interior page graphics © iStockphoto.com/suprun.

Designer: Nicole Russo; Editor: John Murphy;
Photo Researcher: Amy Feinberg